1st Grade Cursive Tracing Practice

Writing Books for Kids

Reading and Writing Books for Kids
Children's Reading and Writing Books

Practice your cursive handwriting by tracing the letters in the alphabet

Aa Bb Cc

Dd Ee Ff

Gg Hh Ii

Jj Kk Ll

Mm Nn

Oo Pp Qq
Rr Ss Tt
Uu Vv
Ww Xx
Yy Zz

Aa

ant

TRACE THE CURSIVE LETTERS,
THEN WRITE YOUR OWN

B b

butterfly

TRACE THE CURSIVE LETTERS,
THEN WRITE YOUR OWN

Cc

candle

TRACE THE CURSIVE LETTERS,
THEN WRITE YOUR OWN

$\mathcal{D}d$

doll

TRACE THE CURSIVE LETTERS,
THEN WRITE YOUR OWN

$$\mathcal{E}e$$

eggplant

TRACE THE CURSIVE LETTERS,
THEN WRITE YOUR OWN

Ff
frog

TRACE THE CURSIVE LETTERS,
THEN WRITE YOUR OWN

Gg

giraffe

TRACE THE CURSIVE LETTERS,
THEN WRITE YOUR OWN

Hh

hamburger

TRACE THE CURSIVE LETTERS,
THEN WRITE YOUR OWN

I i

igloo

TRACE THE CURSIVE LETTERS,
THEN WRITE YOUR OWN

J j

jelly

TRACE THE CURSIVE LETTERS,
THEN WRITE YOUR OWN

K k

kettle

TRACE THE CURSIVE LETTERS,
THEN WRITE YOUR OWN

$\mathscr{L}\,\mathscr{l}$

leaf

TRACE THE CURSIVE LETTERS,
THEN WRITE YOUR OWN

mushroom

TRACE THE CURSIVE LETTERS,
THEN WRITE YOUR OWN

Nn

nest

TRACE THE CURSIVE LETTERS,
THEN WRITE YOUR OWN

orchid

TRACE THE CURSIVE LETTERS,
THEN WRITE YOUR OWN

Pp
penguin

TRACE THE CURSIVE LETTERS,
THEN WRITE YOUR OWN

Qq

queen

TRACE THE CURSIVE LETTERS,
THEN WRITE YOUR OWN

Rr

rocket

TRACE THE CURSIVE LETTERS,
THEN WRITE YOUR OWN

S s

snowman

TRACE THE CURSIVE LETTERS,
THEN WRITE YOUR OWN

$\mathcal{T}t$

tomato

TRACE THE CURSIVE LETTERS,
THEN WRITE YOUR OWN

Uu

unicorn

TRACE THE CURSIVE LETTERS, THEN WRITE YOUR OWN

Vv

vegetables

TRACE THE CURSIVE LETTERS,
THEN WRITE YOUR OWN

Ww

window

TRACE THE CURSIVE LETTERS,
THEN WRITE YOUR OWN

TRACE THE CURSIVE LETTERS,
THEN WRITE YOUR OWN

Yy
yatch

TRACE THE CURSIVE LETTERS,
THEN WRITE YOUR OWN

Zz
zebra

let's try writing each of the following words.

WORD	TRACE	WRITE
hand	hand	
jump	jump	
talk	talk	

WORD	TRACE	WRITE
need	need	
shut	shut	
nice	nice	

WORD	TRACE	WRITE
many	many	
park	park	
door	door	

Visit

BABY PROFESSOR
EDUCATION KIDS

www.BabyProfessorBooks.com
to download Free Baby Professor eBooks
and view our catalog of new and exciting
Children's Books